I0457693

Silkfoot

Silkfoot
Silkfoot
Silkfoot
Silkfoot
Silkfoot

Kent Zimmerman

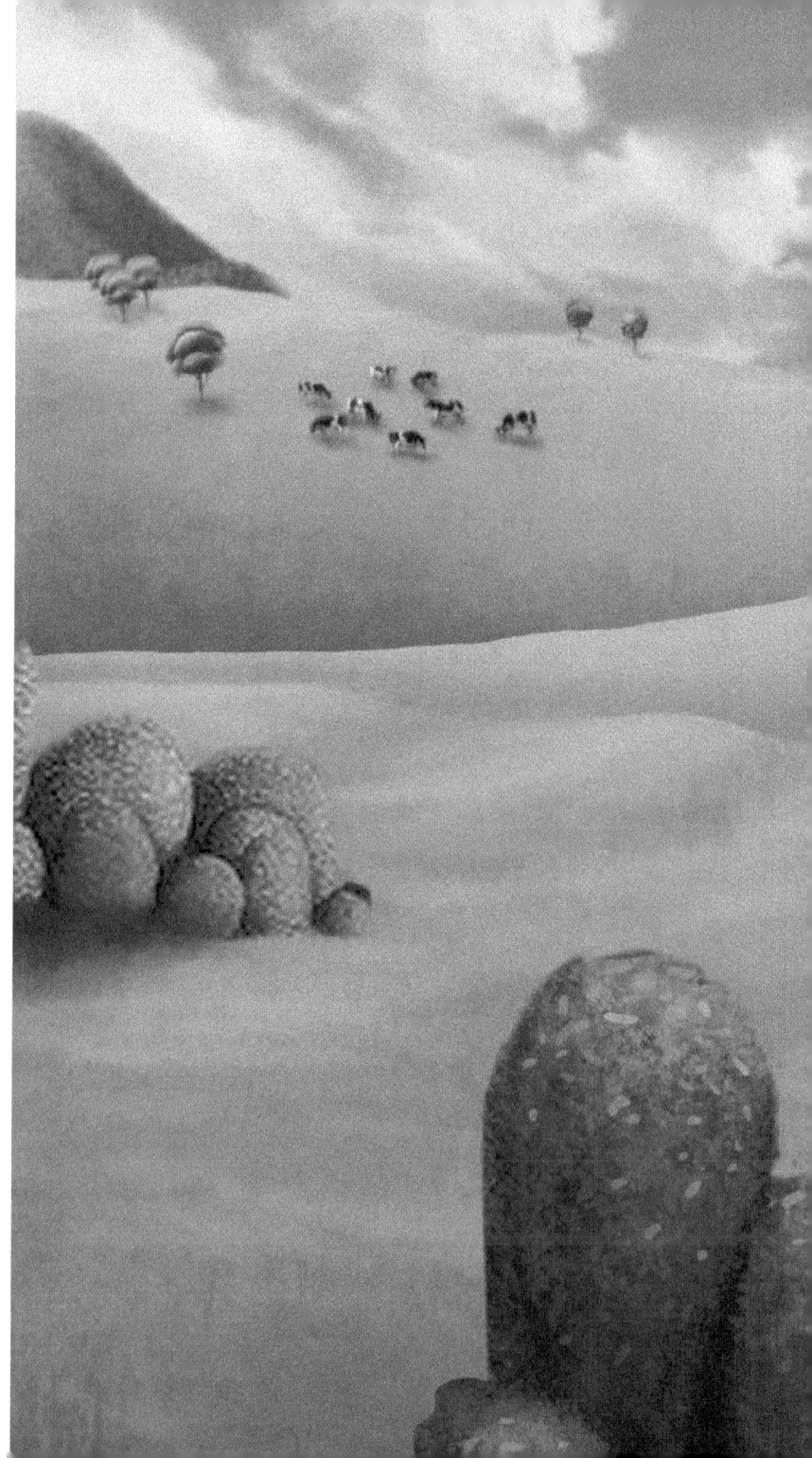

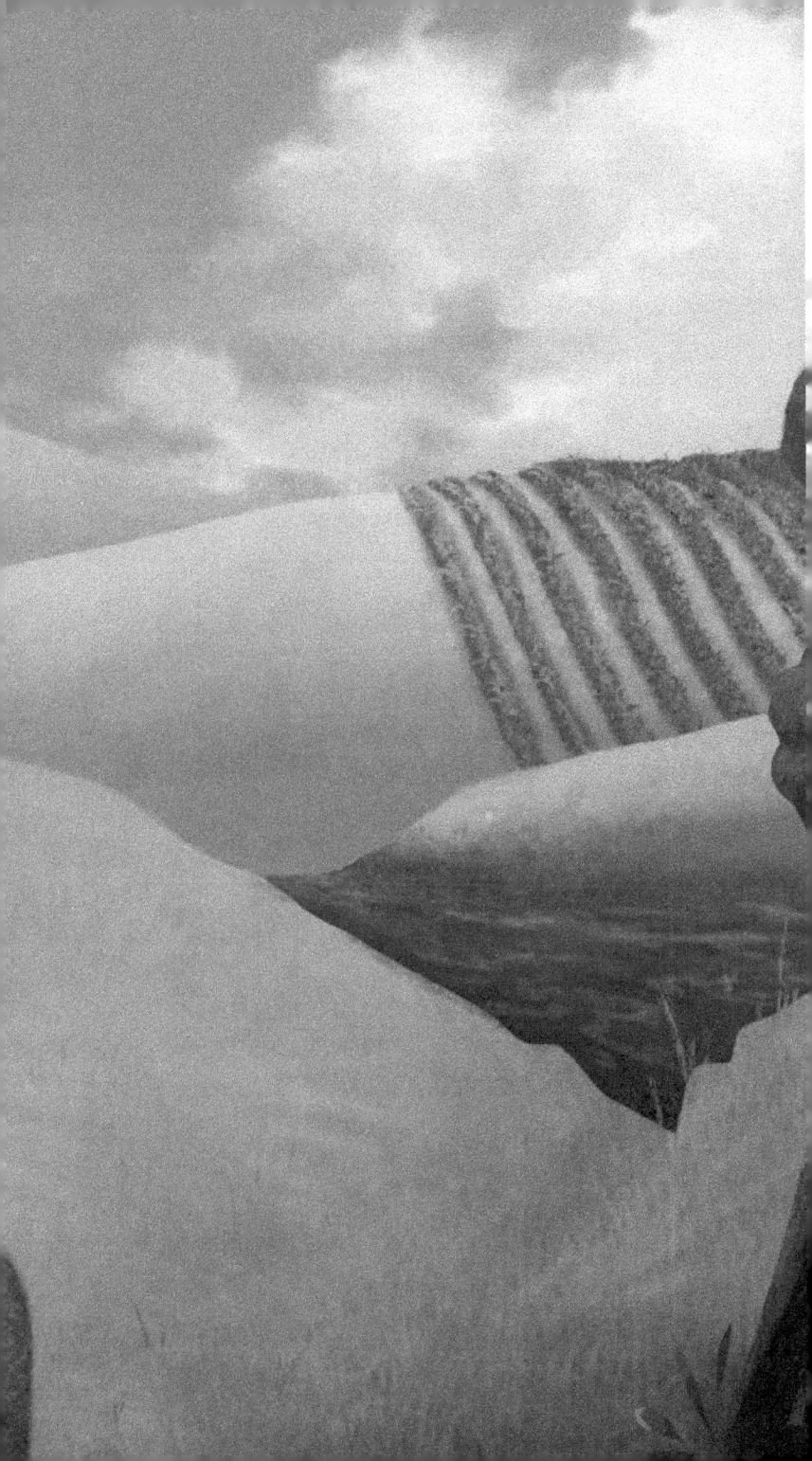

Inquiries and Book Orders should be addressed to:

Great Writers Media
Email: info@greatwritersmedia.com
Phone: (302) 918-5570

ISBN: 978-1-961416-52-9 (sc)
ISBN: 978-1-961416-54-3 (hc)
ISBN: 978-1-961416-53-6 (ebk)

Rev 12/30/2021

Dedicated to my mother Charlene Hope (Wilkerson) Zimmerman and my lovely wife Patricia (Boos) Zimmerman

Silkfoot

She's silkfoot
She toe wise
She knee high
Like sea tides
Like moons rise
Like cool skies
Makes hills slide
Makes nice ride

She's like nice weather

Windup Dream

I was only coasting
Now as a smear
Sweating the changes
As surface
As force
Come to position

Blue stairs in heaven
Leap on out
Jangle the light
As the sky seeps in

Wind up the dream

One thing or another
Open the mouth
Speak out loud

Wind up the dream

Minds in spring
Fruits of the plain

Intensities of reading
Writing the rain

Seeds on the page
Line up the stars

Wind up the dream

Morel

Like morels like poems
Like in the sweetest spots
Like in the truist ways

Morel morel

Ou la la morel

Fa la sancta morel

So so true

I Want

I want
I want to be
Elemental

I want I want
To fire the day
To fire the night
To storm the hill
Make waters run

I want I want
To blow the leaf
The blades of grass
To elevate
A higher state

I want I want
First place and free
A pentacle
A rose red spectacle

I want I want
Enlightenment
Of me

Now Not Waiting

During the last
Demonstration
The line held
Swerves
Into the rough
And fades
Into the dull hill

Murmurs converse
Mothers fathers
Children
All will come

Ripe August fruit
Prepares the question
Which anticipates
The tree and the fall

It's that second look back
That last look at things
That's lost its hold
On space and form

If not in the next one
That big red or blue one
The one we are listening
And looking for

Then let it be this one
One that comes right out
On the horizon
Now not waiting
Though it will fall

Allegory Song

Let this coil
In time
Couple twice
In meter prime

Let rhyme and reason
Riot the seasons
Of artifice
And smiling art

Let rhythm time
Square in rhyme
In fairy tale
And fantasy
In darkest hours
In haloes shine

So ever more
A murmer's breath
On constant shores
To wonder
Ever wonder
This eternal land

The ever painted hills
Stroke the baited brush
The painted walls
In awe of mortal man

So to the arrows mark
The brutes of chalk
Do stare and stare
On breast and brow

So sky it up
Light the day
Still the horizontal high
In song

So sing o muse
Of life and love
In all this earthly bliss
In pleasure fruit
In highest place
So ever life exists

Ones or None

People in roles
The role of the wall
Desk and chair

Which one is more
The desk proper
Or absolute chair

In what sense

What's to say
To some people
Few as the days
And many the ways
Of working
And making mistakes

No one wants to be there alone

Right way or wrong
Evident decisions
Made up transitions
Any movement is good

Wake up awake

Other worlds
One world or another

Setting the curve
Licking at wounds
As waters and sand
Flow down hill

Equal parts
Or one
Count the ways
Stir it up
Or none

Who knows the sound
Of the stars
That goes on in the night
Or what's said to the blue

Or if the mind springs
Beauty and truth
In new day light

No cheap thrills
None to compare
Not one in kingdoms come

In all the eons
All the ones
Or none

Keeps ticking away
Line by line
In the ultimate bound

Plucked wide open

So it begins

Faces

Nothing dreadfull
Nothing receives
Between the soft void

Beyond the finite sum
Beyond monotony
I am
I am not
Alone an existing entity

Death falls off
Abrupt
Arrives on time

Some hypothetical "ism"
Aspires to theory

The moment arrives
Intrinsic

Shadows spring
From the lamp to the wall

We enlighten it

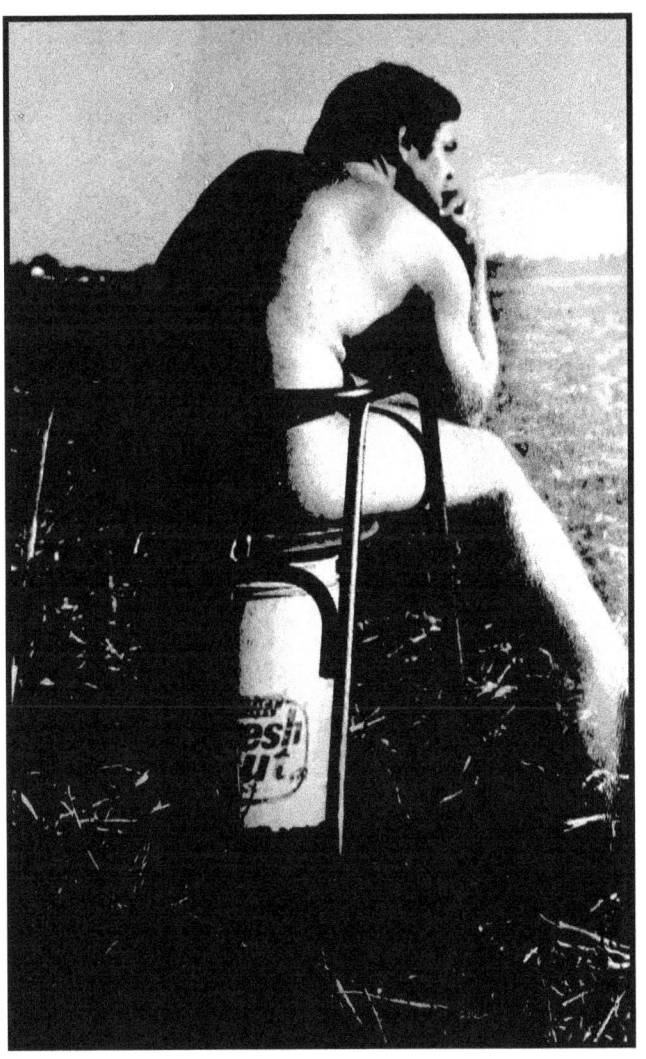

Fresh Cut

Who's to say
What's elementary

Ours to question
Tight lips
Or slip of tongue

Whose lustral cheeks blink
Do the worlds race or slow

Who still lies possum-eyed
Feigns death

Lets angels loose
On hold
Or lets us go

So what goes on
What cuts so fresh
Or blows it up

For all the grain
In all the land
Lest all the powers rest

So lay the stones on high
Rock my displaced soul

Transpose this
This me or I
My displaced self survives
Swears on fate so late
Dignify insult praise alive

To take one step
To walk in Plato's shoe

Go barefoot
On the land

Or revel Buddha wise
Nude and true
With paradise at hand

Who's to argue or judge
What of rights or wrongs
Or what enlightens man

For all the poets' songs
For all the stories told
The question is the quest
For all the world to keep
And all the stars to hold

Chrysalis

On the edge of the post
On the garden gate
The chrysalis emerges
From its protective skin

The spell
Takes a second look back
On the moment
Waxed
In the vulnerable
Instance of migration

Out of the comfort
And finite bounds
Of the lowly past
Our conditional similitudes
Aspire

The soul
By the virgin green
In the new metamorphosis
In the dawn
Awakes

Our destiny
And we can fly

Season

Seasons' fall
Has gladly promised summer
An era of bountiful fruit
And sleeping sums

Outside high tides
Sucked in by sweet tears

Seeds burst
Wide in the rain

Downpour

Giant suns glide the rim
Opens the red door
Intensity steps in

Down with the cool
Hidden
Defined

Then rising
Goodwill pins
Between olives and cherries
Awake and aware

The cool wind whips the glass

I dance inside
Anxiously falling
In coincidence

Crimson walls cry
Beneath the plains
And the opiate of the small hill
Distills the shadow
Of things to come

Hanging Door

Arts' invention head on
Not to remember
Message or mediate
Or how to keep
The rook in drive
Fences in straight lines

Signal or vision
Idea as door
Way in
Way out

The whole carriage
Is there too
Spinning along
A needle in time

Not a slouch
Not a heap
No attitude
The real goods

Shouts out
Orates high and wide
Here and now
Make time
Make perfect place
Make perfect space
Make perfect sense

In perfect spin
Makes up the stars
Makes up the wind
Makes up the mind
Makes up the world

O door
O door

Free

In the aftermath
As the worm fulfills

    destruction
    and chaos

The one yearning
Is a necessity
Especially in wishing it so

The ultimate "rude"
After desire
And dread
Bare open
For the soft leap

Yet still

    we are
           bound

To be free
In the end

A Take Line

We hang tight
Then we get on out
And the weather's fine

And we stand outside
Looking in
Severed by the hand
And the mask
And the glove

Who gets held up here?

I keep on walking
And I talk to myself
Try to be good

I want to give and take

Reflect
On the tell tale lights
In a glassy mirror

The distance recedes
So I start the car
And drive into the fuzzy horizon

Feels so good

Barb Wire

Bright spikes
In a line
Listening
Almost a bridge
To somewhere
Repeating itself
Ever so often

Sharp as the spike
And sharp as the tooth
To bite skin deep
So cool
So bright

Makes me feel
Finite
Makes me explode
Into the Black and White
Shows me the limits
Makes me feel fine

No answers
No calls
Outside the open

Outside walls
Savage and bare

Reaches on out
Interferes
Holds on

Drifting to stop
Instills the lessons
Of the wind
Implodes

Flutters And Waves

In the neighborhood
The houses
Have their own lights
And lives

At dawn
Everyone sleeps
As dreamers walk
The lonesome streets
Looking at the ancient constructions
That built the lives
Of the present inhabitants

The good citizens
Do conform
In similar states
To the world wide view

In passing
Dogs cease their clamor

As dreamers rest
Trees perform
A new dance

Hold shares
With the night
In the public dream

Owl gazes

As light approaches
The sleepers turn over
Into the face
Of collective dawn

Trees perform the new dance
Resumes a public posture

And the vision fades
Into the grays and blues of day
Even the laws behave
Walking down
Lonesome street

Flutters and waves

Loves Song

Where love's the meaning
Love's a song
Real and true

Where love's the angle
Love's the slope
Where love comes through

Where love loves hope
Love loves the sky
Where love is blue

Where love is easy
Love is love
Where love is true

Where love is open
Love loves the stars
Love loves the light

Where love is love
Love loves the sea
Love loves the night

Loves all the days
Loves all the seas
Where lovers nest

Where love is wide
Love loves the brim
Love loves the breast

Where Two loves love
Love loves as One